I0159835

How to Write eBooks & Printed Books
Traditional and Self-Publishing

Jaime Mera

Copyright © 2016 Jaime Mera
All rights reserved.
ISBN-13: 978-1-941336-21-2
ISBN-10: 1-941336-21-3

Preface

❋ --- ❋

I wanted to create this book to help writers and readers of all genres learn about the publishing and writing process. This is for amateur authors, self-publishers, writers wanting to publish in the traditional fashion, and readers who just like to read. This book is a tool for you to learn, enjoy, and hopefully enrich your life for many years to come as a writer and self-publisher.

Each chapter is important and particular to its title. I started with the author information because it is as important as the first and last chapters, and wanted to follow a webpage type of content. You can skip to a particular chapter if you like, but I implore you to read all of the chapters as unique information is in all of them.

This book will show you the process for both self-publishing and traditional publishing. The workings of how your writing needs to be in format and general content. The details of how to write as a style is not covered in depth, because writing like Shakesspear or Edger Allen Poll is not what you need to know when writing or publishing a book. What you mechanically need to know is what should be in your book description, biography, how to pick a title, and how to apply your writing into a style of your own. What you need to know is the process of publishing so it will help you pick the best publishing method, when to publish, and what resources to use for your book. What you need to know is how to improve your writing and storytelling.

Content

Chapter 1

❀ --- ❀

The Author's Information

T he about author section page is suppose to give a snapshot of who the author is and what he/she had to go through to become an author, or it could be a simple biography that relates the author to the reader in a personal or professional way. An example of a bio is below:

Jaime Mera was born in Bogota, the capital city of Colombia. He migrated to the US as a child in 1972. Enlisted in the US Army in 1984 and retired as a Counter-Intelligence Officer in 2008. He attended Indiana University Southeast in 1994 and received a Bachelors of Arts in General Studies with a minor in Psychology. He is currently a student at Seminole State College in Florida. He has been a Christian since 1991, and father of two college age plus children. He published his first Sci-fi novel in 2004, Creator, A Superhero Epic (Series of eight books). His subsequent books of the series include: He Is Known as Ego (2006), Guild Without a Name (2014), The Galaxy Is Ours (2014), and Masterminds (2014). He has also published "Doomsday Prepping and Survival: From Civil Disturbances to Biblical Proportions" (2014) - a doomsday prepper how-to book, and a religious edification book "Jesus and the Paint on the Wall" (2012). His latest publication includes the 6th book of the Superhero Epic series "Superhumans from the Past". Although science fiction is his roots, the genres of fantasy, religion, and practical how-to books are among his favorite interests.

The standard biographical data is very important inside or on the back cover of a book. However, it is written in different ways for different reasons. The biography above is used on the printed book which provides a snapshot of the author and other works. Below is another example of my information which is directed for an audience viewing on Amazon or online which might be displayed in personal author websites. This bio helps tell about the author on a more personal level.

Jaime grew up in Silver Springs, Maryland until the age of twelve, when he moved to Miami, Florida. His most disliked subject in school was English, but when his brother introduced him to Edge Rice Burroughs novels, his love for reading and writing blossomed. His desire to serve in the military motivated him to join the US Army and become an Infantry Soldier. He spent half of his 20 year career overseas, primarily in the Republic of South Korea and Hawaii. Jaime started writing fantasy stories at first, but when computers and self-publishing became available he turned towards science fiction. With a strong foundation in the sci-fi genre, he looked to other interests in religion, how to, short stories and returned to fantasy. Future works include a book about end times prophecy, "Last Days to Eternity", and a fantasy book about dragons and magic, "Calax's World." All books are published in ebook, paperback, and hardcover formats. Available through Amazon.com, Barnesandnoble.com, and Lulu.com. Check out Jaime's author website: www.jaimemera.com and author spotlight at: http://www.lulu.com/spotlight/ SuperheroEpicSeries. or just Google his name on Amazon, or Barnes & Noble online.

You don't have to follow the same styles I have given you; however, there are certain rules you should note. The number one rule is: If you have a positive professional critique like a review or reviews, USE that as the information on the back cover, inside flap, or introduction of an online summary of who you are. You can add personal information if you like to give it a more of a personal touch at the end. Keep in mind that the two examples I gave are not for all my books or online postings. I am currently in the middle of getting two more degrees, Associate of Science in Web Design and Graphic Design. I would use this information for instance in my bio for an author website that I create. I also used this information in the bio for this book because it is important the reader know my expertise on writing and self-publishing.

Each written genre is different and you need to know what to write for each book. I have military and religious seminary experience, so I would focus on that background when putting my biographic data on a doomsday or end times book.

Since I do have five out of an eight book superhero series published, I made sure people know that fact when talking about my achievements as a writer, which is what I did on my first bio example for the superhero book series.

So, in the end; your credentials as a writer, expertise in a subject, or even praise from someone else (besides you) will tell the reader who you are, and what to expect when they do sit down and read your written work. Don't feel bad if you never graduated school or accomplished what most people do in an expected standard middle class family going to college and so on. You are special, and one thing that you should be proud of is that you wrote something on paper; something not everyone does or can do. Telling people your story of where you are from, what inspires you to write, and what makes you a person to be heard is essentially all you need. Reviews and other ideas of how to describe yourself will present itself in time and as your write.

I hope you have written something you like, and not about something you have no interest in or were talked into writing. This in itself usually is related to you who is represented in your bio. As an example: a mother writing about spousal abuse, which will help victims and abusers get the help they need is represented in her bio, or should be. The mother/author should make sure the information is portrayed in a non-bias fashion. Hopefully, the reader will see that the author is not just someone bashing abusive men, but someone who has been in the position and has the credentials to talk about it. It could be a trauma counselor who is the author, or a pastor, and many more people who know about the subject first or second hand. The point of a biography is to give the reader a sense of trustworthiness and connection to a subject that might seem dull but better read because you wrote it.

Perspective and Point of View

Another important note is that the biographic data, summaries of a book, or online information should be written in third person. Try to avoid using first person, like I was born, I published, New York Times hailed me as the best writer of the year. You might think you are being more personal by writing in first person, but you really are not. Strangers who pick up your book, don't know you and when you start with I was, I this, I am; it cuts straight into their personal space from the start and there is a tendency to not want to know you, because you come out to be arrogant or pushy. Famous people can get away with this jump, because the readers that pick up their books (like Oprah Winfrey or OJ Simpson) want them to immediately connect with them in the first person. With a third person perspective of your bio, a reader is eased into knowing you and your work. The story in the book can be first person, and a transcript of a section of your book can be shown on the back of a book in first person. But when it comes to telling someone about you, the "I" is best left out, and replaced by Your First name, his, her, he, or she. If you have more than one author, using both first names would be best as an intro and then use they, them, their, or both.

In the end, you will have to determine when you write first person about yourself. Normally, I write first person about myself when I write how to books, in forums, and at the very back pages of a book, which I call Author Notes. In that section which is usually the very last chapter, I do write as if I were writing a personal letter to you, the reader. Simply, because you will have hopefully read the book and now is my time to be up close and personal, thanking you and telling you how much I hope you enjoyed the story.

Marketing

I talk about marketing in the publishing chapter; however, the biography and book description of your written work is a tool to market not only the story, but you as a writer and subject matter expert of the story for all fiction and non-fiction. It is also the tool you use to help in the keyword search when people browse for books or subjects online. I address the details in the publishing chapter under key words, so just understand that your bio and description of your book is very important for getting information out about yourself and your book.

About My Writing Adventures

I was one year behind in English at sixth grade and hated reading, but when I started to read Tarzan of the Apes, I liked reading. Not because I read it all by myself without someone forcing me to read it. My father obligated me to read Reader's Digest which I hated because I got stuck on many words I didn't know or care to know. However, years later, my brother told me about Tarzan before I read the 23 books, so before I touched the book, I was already interested in the story.

The joy of reading something you like works in making you a better writer. I also liked role-playing games like Champions, Twilight 2000, Dungeons and Dragons, and a few others. I was not one of those people who spent all my time playing games indoor; however, after sixth grade, I enjoyed reading because I got better the more I read. I am still not a speed reader, and like to read slowly compared to the average high school student today. So what am I trying to say?

Reading came first, writing came later. I used the games as a basis for stories or plots. As a game master, you have to come up with stories or plots that the players have never seen before or would not expect. So you have to come up with an entire story from start to finish and figure out possibilities if one player does this or fails to do that. You don't have to be an expert gamer or game master to think about stories, but it helps. Just think of stories and write them down. It might be scribble to someone seeing what you wrote, but to you, it's a master piece in progress.

You can try to write like some authors from scratch and make a story as you write, but that is rare, and it helps to have an idea of what you are writing about. Many authors use outlines, and I will not talk about the details of how to write, since it is covered in the basics page. But for now, back to ideas for your story. Obviously, the more you have read, the more ideas you can come up with. In addition, the more you have seen or heard, like movies and things, the more ideas come to mind. However, you should be careful with this, because I have seen people write a story based on a story that already exists and basically duplicate it without any changes. If you do mirror an existing story, just make sure it has a unique twist or reason.

Okay, back to my writing which started when I was in Hawaii back in 1994. Computers were more or less new at that time and I wrote my fantasy story on a notepad. I transferred the information to the computer, and found out the hard way about backups. I lost eight chapters of my fantasy book called, "Calax's World", twice. One time was because I got the blue screen of death. Anyways, I stopped for a while, and it wasn't until years later when I had the idea of writing my superhero series. I had a better computer, I backed everything up, and had more time to write as I went up the ranks in the military. I wrote the first book, and looked to see how to get it published. I found We-publish and iUniverse. I spent about $2,000 on paying them to create on demand books. They offered a basic marketing system and assisted in creating cover art, which I was very disappointed with. I ended up hiring a local artist to redo the artwork and made iUniverse replace the cover. That was my first published book with a pen name of Alexander B Edwards. Two years later, I wrote the second book, He is Known As Ego. This time I used Author House publishing. I paid $400 for editing from a private editor, and $1,600 to Author House for the rest to include cover art. The artwork was what I requested and have kept it for the 2nd edition of republishing in 2014.

Paying for editing helped, but I found errors after completing the publication, and highly recommend that if you don't pay a lot of money for a professional editor (approx. $800 plus), do your own editing and get friends or family to help you. Today, there are editing programs (like Stylewriter) that can help you greatly, which means you don't have to pay for a professional editor or other services by publishing companies. The same goes with formatting and art work for your cover and inside of the book, if you have art on the inside. Createspace and lulu.com were not around when I published in 2004 and 2006. So when 2012 came around, and I wrote my religious edification book about Jesus, I learned about Lulu and Createspace. I chose Lulu.com over Createspace, and once again, I learned the pros and cons during and after the fact.

The process taught me the process. I figured out that if I do my own formatting, editing, and cover art, then the only cost for a book is the ISBN and the proof. So in comparison to the old way of doing things, I spent $4,000 for the first two books, but for re-publishing the first two and publishing five others between 2012 and 2014, it cost me a total of $600 for 100 ISBNs and seven proofs. Which means that if I write about 35 more books, it will only cost me the cost of a proof per book (roughly $7 to 12 per book, except ebook cost of $1), since I already have the ISBNs for 100 book formats. So for my most recent book "Masterminds", I used Lulu for the hardcover, Createspace for the paperback, and Kindle Direct Publishing (which is linked to Createspace) for my ebook publishing.

Writing is a learning process and a lifestyle. Inspiration comes and goes, but one thing is certain, you need to just write and then write some more. Publishing a book is an obstacle not a tool to help you write your story (unless you are writing a book about publishing), and can be done with a manageable budget. You can spend thousands of dollars with companies, spend many hours convincing an agent to take up your fight to be known, or you can do it yourself with little money and build up until hopefully one day an agent or company will seek you out.

If all fails, self-publishing can become financially satisfying depending on how you market yourself and product online. I personally didn't start out thinking I would write to make money or become famous.

I wrote the books because I wanted to tell the story and give the books to my friends who are a large part of the stories. However, as I grew as an author I realized that I like writing, and know in time it will be successful to a degree when I will get more than what I put into it. I have plans to write short stories, and many more books, until I can't write anymore at the age of 120 or more ☺.

Chapter 2

❋ --- ❋

Writing Basics

Writing is a skill, and knowing how to write needs to be mastered enough so you can focus on the story and not on your writing techniques. It would help if you know what a preposition is or an object and how verbs, adjectives, and adverbs work together. But don't worry, because what you really need to know is how to write a simple descriptive sentence in the correct tense and in the correct point of view.

Below is an example of a tense and point of view:

(past tense and first person point of view)

"The Day I Won"

It was a wonderfully brilliant spring day. The wind was blowing pollen around like wildfire. But that didn't stop my rhythmic breathing as I sped down the final stretch.

Who would have imagined that I would be getting my rights read to me on the side of the road? I mean, Sheriff O'Malley must have been out of his mind. According to him, I was going over eleven miles above the posted speed limit.

I protested of course. How the heck can a person not go faster than the school zone posted limit, even on a bike? I was leading the pack so I must have been going over twenty-five miles an hour. But I had to talk back at him; I mean it was a weekend for God's sake! Who the heck goes to school on the weekend?

When you read the selection, it's clear that its past tense with the use of ed, was, would have, and had. However, when you place dialogue or thoughts of a character, it can be present tense, you just need to make sure what is said is within the quotation marks or italics if it is a thought. Example: I told John, "Take the diamonds out of the box". People sometimes confuse this with present tense, but if you look at how the sentence starts and ends within the period – 'I told' makes the sentence past tense, and the action is present tense within the quotation marks, but is considered part of the same sentence.

The point of view in, The Day I Won, is first person with the use of I, me, and my. The teenager is never mentioned by name in the entire story, but that doesn't matter because he or she is telling the entire story and being named is not a requirement for being first person.

There are two other points of view: second person and third person. It is possible to change points of views in a book or chapter, but it is highly recommended that you do not change points of view in a book, especially within a chapter. The reason is that it will confuse the reader and probably you, and it will mess up any flow in your storytelling. Changing tenses is also highly discouraged. Most books are past tense, primarily because most stories are told in past tense when we talk to people in person. It is natural to talk in past tense on telling a story, and present tense when giving instructions or asking questions. However, in a play or script, present tense is used. This does not mean that you cannot use present tense to tell a story, but it is very difficult and a high degree of skill is needed.

Second person is where the narrator tells you a story, and use the words you, your, or you're is used. A good example is usually in a website, which is second person and present tense. This book is another example as well since I am narrating to you "the reader" and teaching you with instructions, recommendations and stories of the past. In movies it is a narrator who usually starts the movie like in the movie "Dune" which is started by the princess of the Emperor who is narrating. In "Princess Bride", the narrator is the grandfather who is reading the story to his sick nephew. The premise is that the main character is not telling the story, but is one of the characters in the story. Normally, the second person usually doesn't know everything and the story only follows that activity of the main or supporting characters with limited knowledge of what they can only know through their senses and what they find out in the form of gossip, facts, writings, etc.

Third person is where the story is told from an outsider's perspective that is not one of the characters in the story, where the words/pronouns used are: he, they, the name of the character, she, her, or it. Most of my books are third person all knowing point of view. Just to be clear, third person all knowing is Third person. Some people think it is different, only because all knowing allows the author to go into the feelings and thoughts of all the characters in the story. Whichever way you look at the points of views, what matters is how comfortable you are in writing that style and sticking to it for the entire book.

What you don't want to run into is finding out you changed the tenses and points of views without knowing it until after you've written over 5,000 words of storyline. To correct it, you will have to go back and change it to the way you intended, sentence by sentence. If you don't people will be confused as to who is telling the story, what is going on or details of the settings might be completely misunderstood.

Scenes / Chapters: In self-publishing, the written format is geared for 6"x9" page size. Obviously, most people are used to seeing and reading the books in the bookstore that are mostly not 6"x9", but are closer to pocket size. However, the industry is moving to the 6"x9' because it is easy to print and read. On average, a chapter is 5,000-7,000 words, approximately ten pages at a 6"x9" page size. You should not concern yourself too much if you have a 5 or 25 page long chapter, but what you should focus on is a chapter should be as long as it takes to tell a scene. Once the scene changes, it is time to call it a new chapter.

There are exceptions. If you are writing about a long battle for example; you should break it into different chapters by either switching to another scene, on purpose; like in many books and movies who switch back and forth from one group of people to another as action is shown with a cliffhanger before the chapter changes. Or, you can switch the scene within the battle by breaking the battle into two or more sections in a sequence of events.

The name of the chapter should relate to the main idea of the chapter or what I have done is put a memorable phrase in the chapter as a title. Usually the phrase does relate and can help readers remember or find chapter details of the story. A table of content page gives the reader a glimpse of the story; however, what you don't want to do is entitle a chapter with a clear spoiler. An example would be. "The Villain Dies", type of title that gives away the plot or climax. For 'how to books' or 'textbooks', the important part of the chapter should be there as the top key factor for the title.

Audience: If you refer to the story above about the teenager who was pulled over for speeding on a bike, the audience is for teenagers up to men and women aged 60 or less. The entire story is intended to be comical, entertaining, and children friendly. What you should consider is not only the audience, but usage of words for that audience. Profane language is of course at your discretion, but at the same time, you will limit your audience and publishing company if you use the "F", "B", "A" words, and a few more colorful words all throughout your writing. There are written works which are placed in the adult only area, but you don't want to fall into that pool if you want a larger audience population. In my case, I avoided the "F" word, by saying "What the…" You can write things without the use of profane language and should make it a point to be able to write descriptively without vulgar verbiage. This also goes for describing sensual or violent scenes in a graphic way that is repulsive. I described the assassination of a mother and daughter by a shotgun blast full of poisoned fletches. It is gruesome, but not so graphic that it is so repulsive to most readers that they would stop reading and not continue.

I have had a reader tell me that my fifth book in the superhero series was turning dark, probably because many people died with gun shots to the head, and she stopped reading. Even thought there is a happy ending in the book; that one reader turned away because of the amount of violence told. What is important is that your writing does not turn away all your readers. If you look at movies, many show massive destruction of city blocks or entire cities, but it is not so graphic that you see people dying an agonizing death. For example, in the movie "Man of Steel", Superman and

General Zod destroyed many buildings, and many had people in or around them. Thousands of people died, but almost none were shown because it was made for a wide audience, managing to be rated as PG13. So what your audience will think about, what happens in the story or how you describe your story matters on how you will attract and maintain a certain type of audience.

Story development: I try to have comedy, romance, action, and mystery all rolled up into one story of my superhero series. It is easy to do if you have the right elements. The basic characteristics of a story are a protagonist (the hero or main character), antagonist (villain or resistant character, or situation), and a problem which can be the crisis or end goal. A crisis could be fighting off an alien invasion or end goal could be the main character winning a competition. With those three things, you write your story. You can make an outline and fill in the blanks of how the three fit together to create the buildup and climax to an ending that leaves the reader with a conclusive satisfaction, but still wanting to read more. In most cases it's for writing more books on the same storyline. As for chapters, you want to end a chapter with the reader wanting to know what's next, usually this is done with a chapter ending with a new crisis or problem popping up.

You might have heard this before, "don't tell, show the story." Using action words and adjectives is important in all your writing. Below is an example of a situation told two different ways: Instead of telling how the police or why the parents didn't press charges, show the reader by describing the action with dialogue by the police and parents.

Telling

David burnt the boat into submission, floating its last on the pier's edge. John and Wendy were confounded as to why their son would carelessly start a fire by smoking and drinking in secret. It was parental denial to the fact that it was probably the only spot that was private while the boat was left alone at dock on the weekdays. When the police arrived, they were also powerless to arrest the minor as the only proof of illegal activity was a scared teenager's whimpering confession in a state of denial of suspected drug use.

Showing

"My son will not last a minute in jail." Wendy fearfully signed.

"Don't worry darling, the boat's insured, and it seems he's learned his lesson." John comforted her as David trembled and whimpered in the back of the squad car.

"If you are not willing to press charges, we can't hold your son, but I would recommend he get some counseling. Teenagers are being exposed to many over the counter drugs, and addictions are rising in the community." Officer Patterson handed them a list of drug rehab and adolescence counseling centers.

Word Usage: The more descriptive and action words you have, the better. Just make sure you don't have an overload of complex words. Complex words are those vocabulary words that many people don't know or remember. Comprehension is important for a reader to be satisfied with your writing. If the vocabulary is too simple, it will seem childish, unless the written work is intended to be a children's book. If the vocabulary is too hard (or complex), then the reader might learn new words, but more than likely the flow of the story will be lost along with interest, since the reader will be trying to figure out what is being said on every paragraph.

There are software programs on your computer like grammar, spell check and a thesaurus. They are okay for writing an email to someone, but for a long story, they're not enough. Grammar check will not find the difference between bare, bar, bear, fair, pair, and many more words that grammar check or spell check will not catch. There are two solutions. Eyeball editing. You and someone else reading and correcting. The second is a program like Stylewriter, which is free and does catch grammar errors like the ones I mentioned. It also tells you if you have complex words, long sentences, and recommends words that will improve your writing. Find a program that works for your budget if you want to spend money on it. Otherwise, download free programs to help you write and edit your work in a relatively quick manner.

Formatting: The formatting of your writing is important from the start. I was taught to place two spaces after a period back in the 70 and 80s. Today, I hope you have been taught to place only one space after a period. If you have been taught incorrectly or have habits that are now not proper in writing, I recommend you get in the right habit of doing things, like placing only one space after a period and properly indenting without using the tab key. But note: for an eBook format, if you want an indent you must use the tab or em space for that particular indent.

You need to know how to write a dialogue by using the correct use of quotation marks, italics, underlining, hanging letter and indention. I have mentored people, and they started by just writing things out, without putting proper punctuation and quotation marks. You need to punctuate correctly, or you will end up performing a massive editing session to correct the issues later. Quotation marks are used to place dialogue, get in the habit of using them if you haven't used them before. As for when to use them? You can write:

"I ate the pie." Sally joyfully mumbled, wiping her mouth.

Or start with:

Sally gladly wiped her mouth proudly saying, "I ate the pie."

Either one is correct, and it depends on how your style of writing is or develops. I tend to start with dialogue first, then the description. Whichever way you chose to write, make sure the flow of the message is not lost. So try to stay consistent by starting with dialogue first most of the time or vice versa. Note I said most of the time and not all of the time. Sometimes you should change the order so that emphasis is made on the action or dialogue.

If you're writing dialogue between two people, you should introduce who is talking with a name, and as long as the speakers don't change, you don't have to say who is talking because natural progression is to go back and forth in a dialogue. However, if you do have a name you can attach a description to the dialogue, and you should keep that in mind.

"What's going on here?" John screamed.

"The fan broke in half!" Peter innocently raised his shoulders and hands.

"I warned you not to let him out of the cage." John unplugged the fan's cord.

"But, Dad, I didn't. I swear!"

"So how did he get out?" Twitty chirped mercy next to Peter's shoes, John staring him down.

"He picked the latch with his beak."

As you can tell, there's an indentation on all the new dialogue or paragraphs. Make sure you indent after the first paragraph of a chapter; otherwise you will be viewed as a poor writer. Indenting makes for a clear and smoother flow of information where the reader can tell who is talking, and when a new paragraph or dialogue begins and ends. If you are writing on a website, indenting is not necessary and is not looked at in a negative way. However, indenting a story should be done even on a website so readers can track the story better OR at the very least there should be a blank enter/return space, known as a hard return, between the changes in dialogue or paragraphs.

What I have talked about is enough for you to get started in writing a book. If you are learning or plan on writing a play or movie script, it's a little different than the average book on the shelf. Also, if you're writing a technical book or a comic, it's different, and my recommendation is to do research online to see the standards and various methods for writing each.

Margins are different for all publishing companies, but not too different. The average inside book margin for a 6" x 9" book is .25" for top, bottom, and outer page, and between .35" for 300 pages to .75" for 600-800 pages on the inside page. The reason for this different range of margin is when a book has more pages and the book is opened, the inside page cannot be fully exposed with a book for instance that has 600 pages as compared to one with 100 pages. So the formula is sound and you can also look at companies with their margin recommendations like Createspace which give you margins for different sized books (pocket size to very large size) and exact number pages that will alter the spine letter size of a book. The problem is that they tell you what it should be, and don't give you a workable template that you can edit or save. My best recommendation is to experiment with the margins to include cover size margins and bleeds. I found a MS word document template as a free download that some other writer created. This template was a practical solution so I didn't have to recreate the wheel. It had the set margins for the copyright page, numbering system, headers and footer presets, and hanging letter. Remember that the margins I gave you earlier is so the printed information is not printed too close to the edge of the pages, which will show if you mess up the margins. If you do make the margins too small or large, you will hopefully see the error in your digital review, instead of the actual printed proof before you go final in the publishing process. I used the word document template for my previous books; however, I highly recommend you use InDesign or similar layout program. InDesign is probably the best thing to use for writing your book, because it gives you an easy way to make the formatting you want and need, in addition to text and images you may want to place inside and outside your book. If you are not InDesign savvy, then go with what is easiest for you which for many PC users is a Word Document, and there are several editors for Mac users like Google docs, Pages, iA Writer, Myword and a few others.

As for the font size and typeface, I would recommend you look at the top 10 most liked and read typefaces by readers. I choose Minion Pro which was on that list as number three. Number one when I last looked was Garamond. Letter size is 10-12 point. I used size 12, except for the list of characters where I used 11 point for those pages. For the hanging letter, I used 72 point, and **Palatino Linotype**. For the chapter letters and chapter titles I used different sizes, ranging from 29 to 36 and **Agency FB** typeface. I recommend you take a close look at the books you like and use them as a basis for your choices of sizes, chapter setup, header setup and so on. Keep in mind that many of the books in bookstores use traditional publishers who have access to more typefaces and styles like chapter names in the header for each particular chapter. However, with Adobe InDesign you can do the same or better.

In addition, when you publish an eBook, there are a limited number of fonts allowed. So if you have a font like 12 Agency FB, the publishing system used by Kindle Direct for instance, will not accept it and automatically change it to **Times New Roman**. If you wrote your eBook or converted all the font to **Times New Roman**, **Garamond**, **or Arial,** then you should be fine because the computer system (publisher) will not automatically change the font on you. If you haven't noticed; all of this paragraph is in 12 point size and the actual fonts are seen different even though they are all 12 point. Garamond, Agency FB and Times New Roman are smaller than Arial. What does this mean? Not much of anything except that you need to decide how big you want your text in your book. The larger the size of text, the more pages you will have and probably makes it easier to read for the average reader. The smaller the font which should not be less than size 10, the less pages your book will have and probably harder to read, except for eBooks which can be zoomed in or out. The more pages you have, the more it will cost the reader to get in their hand and a little more royalty for you. However, the less a book costs, there will be a higher chance of more readers buying your book. So there is a balance and it should be your focus to give the reader a pleasurable experience by having clear comfortable sized fonts. I recommend a serf font (like **Minion Pro** or **Garamond**) for paper text and eBooks, and san-serf font (like Arial or MS Reference Sans Serif) for web.

Spacing: The spacing I used in my books is 6pt before and 6pt after, line space of exactly 17 pt, snap to grid, and justified for body of text. Centered for titles, and left or right alignment for intro or setting text determined by where the outer margin is / outer page. I played around with spacing and found that particular setting to my liking because it didn't clutter the words and didn't spread the words or lines too much which made it easy on the eyes. For those who want to get technical, I am talking about tracking and leading of fonts and paragraph settings. You can look at your digital manuscript and think it is okay, and you would be right to a point. When you get your printed proof you will see exactly how it comes out when not on a computer screen. But you don't have to wait entirely for a printed proof of a book. You can print a page out on your printer and have an idea of how it will look. Print the page according to a 6" x 9" size page and it will be as accurate as you can get it before the printed proof. Experiment or use the settings I suggested. I will talk more about the book covers in the publishing chapter, and I hope this information has been of value to you so far.

Chapter 3

❀ --- ❀

Tools

Shakespeare said it best in a play, "Can one desire too much of a good thing?" (As You Like It - Act IV, Scene I). If your writing style is good, then there is no such thing as too much of a good thing. However, if you have no exposure, your book cover is not attractive, your title is misleading, the book content is hard to read, or your story is unbelievable or too predictable, chances are you are not using the correct tools for your reader to enjoy a good thing.

Tool 1: A Reliable Computer with Proper Software

The first and most important tool is a reliable computer that can run the latest Microsoft Word software, acrobat, and internet browser, plus at the very least be able to use PowerPoint or better software like Photoshop, Illustrator and InDesign. You will need to be able to create word doc and pdf files, to include creating imagery. Self-publishing companies require submissions in specific ways. For example, a submission of a manuscript to Createspace must be submitted as a pdf file. Images submitted must also be as a jpg. So if you create your book on Word and use Photoshop you have to convert it into a pdf and save the image(s) as a jpg(s). (PDF stands for Portable Document Format and JPG is Joint Photographic Experts Group) A computer is a must, which replaces the old fashion way of writing on a typewriter.

In the old days, the standard was to use a typewriter, 12 Courier font, double spaced, and 1 inch margins for a manuscript you had to mail to your prospective publisher with a cover letter. If any of these specifications were not met, the publisher would toss it at first glance like a badly made resume cover letter, and not bother to let you know if they even looked at it or what was wrong with it. You would think that with computers and online technology, traditional and self-publishing would now be easy and quick.

Yes and No. As the writer, using a word document and submitting things online is easier, Spell check, grammar check and literature software makes even the weak writer, a semi-strong writer. Publishers just put in the digital data and print out a complete book within a day or at the most, several days. So why isn't it easy? Volume is something that the writer and publisher have to deal with everyday. Since almost everyone has a computer or access to a computer, a written work is created everyday by many people. Traditional publishers tend to still use mailed in manuscripts or only look at short files consisting of the first three to six chapters of a work. In addition, traditional publishers will only talk to literary agents. This weeds out many written works that are not bestseller material, sort of speaking. This is a business, and if a traditional publisher feels that your written work will not produce a certain amount of money in a given amount of time, they would rather skip you and find someone that will have a higher chance of making them fast, consistent and a lot of money.

Self publishing companies are a little different. In many ways, companies like Createspace, Kindle Direct, and Lulu.com, want you to succeed. Even if you sell nothing with only buying one proof, they make money, and the amount of money they spent on helping you out is almost none or positive on their end. Their helping you self-publish also makes you a better writer for future possible sales and if you are successful, they make money along with you. They focus on mass producing works from a larger author pool, than the traditional publishing companies that focus on publishing with a moderate to high return author or prospect. In addition, traditional publishing companies are now using online publishing as a way of cutting costs, and marketing profit on the digital side, keeping up with future trends.

Tool 2: Useful Websites

You can make a long list of websites that say they help in writing, tutorials, and services – like book covers and editing. There are websites like Scribophila which is a website where you will find amateur and professional writers who post their work for people to critique as peers, and groups who actually help you in writing and publishing. But like most websites, this one in particular requires that you read someone's written work and critique it. There is a point system and the more points you collect, the more written work you can post to get a critique. It is nice if you have a professional or very good writer who can critique your work, but this is not always the case. If you have the time to read other people's work and critique it, this site might work well for you. If not, then you might end up getting a critique like, that was bad or it didn't make sense. In other words, if someone who is bias or doesn't know how to write, they will be critiquing your work and taking up a spot of someone with quality feedback that could have been given to you. I placed several of my already published work in the queue, and found out as I already knew, that everyone has their own opinion as to how you should write your story. So if you do get into a social website that gives you feedback on your work, you need to listen to it, throw out the non-sense, consider what sounds reasonable; and accept any constructive information on how best to write or publish your work. One thing you do need to consider is if your written work is getting good responses from other then your family, then it is probably good enough for publishing, and all you need to do is improve on top of an already good product.

One thing I like about social websites that give you feedback is you do get a chance to see good and bad writing, to include how people think about other people's writing. You can see bad writing and tell who is new with many grammar errors, little description, little action words, or who writes with passion, but has no direction with a plot(s) that breaks the action or story. On the other side, you see the very good writers who have not hit the bestseller, and should be there, but lack of exposure which has kept them hidden among the millions of books per year, lost in the system. Hopefully you are one of these writers or soon to be famous writer. I recommend you surf the web and find your useful sites, converting them to favorites or bookmarks. Below is a small list of examples of websites I found useful in my learning experience.

Authorconnect.com: http://www.authorconnect.com/. This site is needed for you to register your written work. Registration is not all that important, but it sort of is if you are worried about copyright. The registration is free and sort of places your work on the board without having to publish or get an ISBN. The reason you will need an ISBN is to sell your work, not for copyright purposes alone. Anything you come up with and put on paper/digits is inherently copyrighted to you the creator, but registering it will give it a time stamp sort of speaking. On this site, you can talk to and find other authors, but most importantly, you can connect with and find agents. You can contact the agents that specialize in your genre and with some luck, your work will be picked up by an agent. This is not a guarantee that you will get a traditional publisher, but it is a good start into traditional publishing. Self publishing is nice, but with traditional publishing, you can jump in leaps and bounds in becoming a bestseller.

Fiveer.com: links you to book cover artists and editors; however, it can be expensive and the cheaper options as low as $5 for one book cover might give you a final product that is not top quality or to your full satisfaction. If you don't have Photoshop or something similar, or know someone who can create your book cover art, then I would recommend you look at this site or others like it to create your art work. I will add that you will probably need to supply stock photos for your cover, otherwise the artist can do it, but will charge you extra for it. There are also artist that can draw your art work, which once again will cost you. Having said that, the cost of using artists on sites like this is cheaper than using the self-publishing company services in lulu.com or createspace for art work, which can run as high as $4,000 for a custom made book cover.

Dailywritingtips.com: this site is a collection of everything a writer might want; like 1,000 facial expressions, used in your descriptions of characters or animals. This site covers many areas of writing improvement and gives you access to proper word usage.

Royalroadl.com: provides writers a way to show off their work without a point system. This site focuses on fantasy writing and posts works from established renowned authors and new writers. Very friendly environment and you get decent feedback. The only drawback is that you post small sections of writings and your posts will be bumped off the list as other posts are made. So there is a tight window of your writing been shown, But if you post your writing, chapters, in sections, this will give you good exposure and usually some useful feedback.

Writeaboutdragons.com: YouTube tutorial for writers, very impressive and extensive class lectures by a bestseller writer and professor. YouTube is all you need for this and the lectures will definitely improve your storytelling and writing style.

Bowker Identifier Services: https://www.myidentifiers.com/get-your-isbn-now: This site is a required website to have, especially if you are buying your own ISBNs. I use it only to obtain ISBNs, but they supply other things like widgets and barcodes. You can also publish with them by putting your work in a database. Most of these services are for publishing companies or businesses that have a large inventory. However, this site is for individuals (non-corporate entity) as well, so I highly recommend you check this site out and use it accordingly.

A good search engine in general will be your best friend. This is where you do your research when talking about things in your book or written work. You can use other resources like books in a library, but just google-ing something is so much easier. Talking to subject matter experts can also help greatly in this. My brother is an aerospace engineer and has worked on many aircrafts to include military jets for over a decade. It was from talking to him, that I was able to confirm the way a plane would react if an explosion created a hole on the fuselage of a Boeing 747 at 40,000 feet. So when I wrote about a high-jacking gone bad in "Guild Without a Name, A Superhero Epic" series, it's believable/realistic, considering it is a sci-fi story with superheroes and crazy powers. But in the end it told the story in a smooth and believable fashion which is what you want your reader to take away when it comes to storytelling.

Tool 3: A Good Editing System

I found the latest version of Stylewriter, which is a program that you can link to your document and it will tell you everything you should consider when editing your work. It provides the common spelling and grammar correction, but also length of sentences, proper vocabulary usage, paragraph and sentence structure, and recommended word usage for easy reading. The average length a sentence should be is about 8-12 words, and you will notice that your sentences are sometimes as large as 30 words. You can change the words and sentences according to the program's recommendations or not. There are other similar programs, but some cost money, some have a word maximum limit which means you can only edit 5,000-10,000 words at a time, and some only work online. So if you go off to a secluded spot to get away from it all, it would help to have a program that is independent from the Internet.

The other practical editing tool is another person who likes to read. People that like to read tend you give you good feedback, and catch errors easier. I use my friends and brother who like to read and for a lack of better words, by brother is my best devil's advocate. Since my brother is in the family, I expect him to tell me the good and the bad. That is not the case for every family member. So whoever you find, make sure they cover all areas. Having someone tell you that there are no errors and the book was great is pointless if that person can't tell you why it was good or bad, and how to maybe improve your written work. My brother and I got into a lot of discussions about the subplots and character development in my books, and I did change maybe 20% of descriptions or action. The rest of his and other's input I considered, but put aside and stood by what I wrote. This helps you justify why you wrote what you wrote. My brother also caught a lot of grammar and spelling errors. A lot to me is maybe 50 or more errors out of a 90,000 word book. If you don't get every error, that is okay, even bestsellers have errors. The idea is not to have one or more errors on every page or a few pages. This becomes distracting to readers, and you will get those attention to detail people (like your critics) who look out for things like errors and that is all they talk about or focus on. Unlike a fan who just wants to find out if the hero saves the day, gets his/her true love, or the villain gets away with it or not. In addition, these personal editors need to also give you feedback on your artwork. Hopefully, they have a good eye, and can tell you how to improve or correct your book cover(s) or illustrations inside the book. If you have access to Photoshop and other Abode programs, I highly recommend you use the programs. YouTube on how to use the programs if in doubt. You can pay as a non-teacher or student around $40-50 dollars a month to use all of the programs without having to pay for the program for life which is in the thousands. Knowing how to use these programs will save you a lot of time and money trying to create your artwork. If you are a student you can get the Adobe Creative Cloud suite for $20 a month. If you don't want to use the programs you stop the subscription and restart it whenever you do need the software. This is for the latest versions of the programs. It is possible to get the older versions for less money or under the table sort of speaking, and still be able to create very good artwork. If you don't get savvy with these programs, at the very least Adobe Photoshop, then you will end up paying someone else to do it for you which can be cheap or very expensive depending on who you contract or know.

Tool 4: Other People's Books

I recommend you go to the mall and find a bookstore. Go directly to the bestseller rack and pick up books. Look at the covers and introduction pages. Read the first page of the first chapter. Then jump around to the next book. Once you looked through half a dozen books, go to the section of your genre. Pick up books there. Keep note on how authors structured their books. What was said on the back, in the inner flap, artwork, format of the page, table of content, and writing style. You will see something interesting. Not all of the bestseller authors can write very well. Chances are you will find one or two errors on the first page or back cover in one of a dozen books. Not just errors, but writing that is confusing or is clearly nothing but babbling. You will see things that other people will tell you never to do, like write long and almost impossible to pronounce names of characters and places, or have similar or identical names for characters. You might have done this; but what you should take away from this is: find the one author you would love to emulate. I am not saying copy that author, but study why that author's writing/storytelling is powerful and liked by you. I have read many books, and even though I like Piers Anthony, Ann Rice and many others, out of all the authors, Tom Clancy is (to me) one of the best writers around. It is not what he writes about, it is how he writes it. Since I have military experience, you might say that I am bias, but not true. I know what he talks about in detail, but he explains it in such a smooth and simple way, at the same time describing the story so well that he shows you instead of telling you the story. If I were to write the same storyline, I would put words that confuse people or write so the flow of the story is like trying to read a technical manual in the middle of a fire fight. So the intent is to learn to write with a style that is part of you and part of an excellent writer who has his/she work already exposed to the public.

I talked about looking at other people's writing on websites and you could just go online and look at books. However, this method works best when you look at a solid book up close. Of course solid books are different than digital screens, and so is ink on paper. Reading the text on a paperback and hardback book is different, simply because different paper is used for each format and ink prints differently on a particular type of paper or type of printer used. A stronger white background on black ink tends to be easier to read, and is used on hardback books. The quality of paper depends on the cost of printing a book which tends to give paperback books an off white background. Seeing the book in hand and focusing on the author of your liking will help you know or set the bar for what your book goals should be once you publish.

The last note is on thumbnails and cover art. When your book is advertised online, your cover art needs to be seen clearly and quickly give the prospective reader an interesting image to include text that is easy to read. If the art or text is confusing or hard to see because of bad color usage or size, it will be passed along and another book will be looked at. If you look on Amazon and surf through the normal list of books, they are displayed as small thumbnails. The ones that catch your eye, should be how your art work and text measure up to. This is a simplistic way of explaining how your book cover should be attractive, and I suggest you look at a book called, "Make a Killing on Kindle". It will explain how marketing works online and how to best expose your book to the world. I will cover many of these methods used in the book, but not go into all the specifics. My intent is not to focus on marketing alone which will be a book by itself, but keep in mind that all this information is not all inclusive or guaranteed to produce results in any one book or website. This is one reason I wanted to make this book short and to the point, with enough information to answer questions, and guide you in the right direction if not specifically answered in this book.

Chapter 4

❀ --- ❀

Self Publishing

I f you have the money and don't want to format your story, create the cover, and/or edit the story, then what you want to do is find the self-publishing company that will help you the most for the best use of your dollars. There's a lot of information online about companies, like iUniverse, Createspace, Lulu, Mindstir Media, Notion Press, Bob Books, Lightning Source, and about thirty more. SO which one do you pick?

I would go down all of the companies on the list which you can find on Wikipedia online. Some companies only focus on certain genres, some companies only publish one or two formats. Some companies offer premium packages that seem like it will turn you into a bestseller. Beware, the services might seem nice, but once the service is over, you can be left alone with a really nice book and very few sales. An example of this is when a company offers a marketing package of $450, you will get 200 business cards, information on how to write to radio stations to get an interview that is broadcasted on the air, and a critique from a reputable reviewer. You pay this money and get a 3 star review, and have to sell yourself with a radio station for one sitting, or hope that giving out business cards 24/7 will do the trick. In the end, you will have probably ended up spending a lot of money with little return. But of course, the more money you put into it, the more services you can get which may probably give you a return. This can cost you $4,000 to $15,000 for a well edited, great cover, and well made marketing system that works without you having to sell yourself 24/7. The problem is money, and if you don't have over $10k, the only other route is to self-publish with a company that offers the best at a budget you can manage.

I can only tell you from experience how I published seven books for the price of about $700 and intend to publish five more for an extra $100 with Lulu and Createspace. Don't get me wrong. I spent over $4,000 on my first two books when self-publishing first started in early 2000s. And I learned my costly lesson for two books which well still haven't given me a return over what I spent. You of course do not have to publish so many books, and if your intent is to publish one or two books as an experiment, it will cost at least $120 or more to publish one book. Whether you buy your own ISBN or get a free company provided ISBN, it will cost around $100. The catch is you will have to format, edit, and create your own book cover. You can get someone to make a cover for cheap, but that is not where the cost is. The cost is for the ISBN or the company's required cost which can either be an ISBN that is around $90 and the proof of the book. Lulu has a free ISBN, but you can only sell through them on their website, so it does not go to Amazon or Barns and Noble, so less exposure. On the same token, Createspace provides an ISBN which is cheaper than the normal universal ISBN, but once again you are limited through their distributors and you cannot take your book and distribute it on another platform without their permission. This is why I bought the universal ISBN through Bowker Identifier Services.

Now, there are companies that offer to do all of the publishing things involved if you can convince them that your book is a bestseller or fall into what they are looking for. This is different than an agent. The companies offer assistance, like Web Publish, Be Happy. This company helps aspiring photographers who are trying to publish their book or photo work. The company has resources like workshops to help in the process. There's a lot of free online assistance, but the actual printed book is what you want to end up with if not at the beginning.

I say this because it's easy and cheap to publish an ebook with Kindle Direct Publishing (KDP). A short book 20 or more pages can turn out to be your platform to getting that $10k and publish a larger book and get more royalties and expertise. It could be a simple book like how to make memorable Christmas cards or your family cooking secrets. Just make sure it is written well and is something readers can use to enrich their lives, thoughts or feelings.

The Process: Each company has a process, and you can just follow the instructions. However, I learned that until you follow the process, you really don't know what to expect until you do it or pay for the service. It is okay if you just jump into it, but I will tell you what happened with me so you won't be caught completely off guard. Below is the process I went through with Createspace and Lulu.

First: I created an account with both of them after I had a finished manuscript. If the book is not finished to include the book cover, you will have an account and cannot complete the final publishing process. But at least you will have an account. It does not cost you any money until you assign an ISBN or buy one from Bowker Identifier Services. The good thing is the account is free to have and the information you upload is saved. So if you upload the finished or unfinished manuscript, it will be there, and if you need time to make the book cover, you have time to upload it later and complete the process.

Second: Whichever way you go, in the end you will need the completed manuscript (edited and formatted). Or if you want to use their services for editing and formatting, all you need is the completed story, and a finished book cover or good idea for the book cover art. You will also need to have a summary and biography ready which is limited to a certain amount of words, which is dictated by the amount of space on the back cover and/or inside flap, and the company's max word limits. In the summary which is filled online, there is between a 400 to 1000 word limit, depending on the publishing company. Use every bit of it, especially on Amazon.com descriptions. The keywords that you pick needs to be in that summary and the more words in the summary that overlap, the more hits it will get when a search is started by a potential reader on a search engine.

In addition, if you want a photo of yourself on the back cover, you need to have that available to upload. Color or black and white photos is not a factor, you just need a clean and clear 300dpi photo that does not present you as a person who is childish or left winged (bias). This means not posing with a clown or weird facial expression or wearing copyrighted material like a Star Wars T-shirt. If you created a unique logo, you can wear it, but it's not worth the effort to get permission to wear someone else's logo or brand. Many authors have their photo in black and white wearing a smile with a nice neutral background. That is really all you need, but you can get creative and pose yourself on top of a tank if your book is about armored vehicles, for example. Whatever you do, I recommend you look at other author photos if you are clueless as to whether you want to or still have questions as to how to pose in a photo for a book. The photo is also for your author photo on Amazon and other sites, so keep in mind that your photo is not just for the book alone. You don't have to have a photo at all in the beginning, but it would be good to put one online so when you do get followers and your fame increases, you won't have to get one at the last minute. Also, the photo is used for advertising for many publishing companies and it does present you as a professional author.

Third: You need to know how much money you plan to price your book for selling your book. There is a minimum amount that you must sell each format, and the publishing company will tell you how much royalty you will get for a specific format with their calculators. You have the final decision on how much over the minimum you desire to sell your book. There is an ideal price for a book and I recommend you look at your genre and make it not too cheap and not too expensive, compared to others. When you go through the distributor information, is when you will put how much the book will cost. Pay attention to all the information the online fields ask for. If you don't want to put exact information, like number of pages, you don't really have to. However, it will be better in the long run to have as much detail as possible so it is displayed on Amazon fully. It is recommended that eBooks go for $2 to $4 range which many readers get simply because it is cheap. You could sell a 300 page ebook for $6.95 and chances are that they will sell a little less, simply because the same genre books are overwhelmed with books that are cheaper. If you already have a large reader pool, then selling for regular prices will be better in the long run. Look at the competing book prices and decide. You can change the price, but it will usually require you to get a different ISBN, or you can add price cuts at the expense of some of your royalty which does not require you to change the ISBN or republish. If you decide to change the pricing before you approve the final proof, you can without any issues. As a rule of thumb, it is best to follow their steps to make changes before and after you approve your final and publish.

Fourth: Make sure you have your keywords. The name and title of the book is automatically placed in your keywords search. SO if your title is for example: The Best Way in Constructing Log Cabins. Your keywords **should not** be [best, way, constructing, log, or cabins] because they are automatically placed in the keyword search, and all you are doing is duplicating the words and wasting the number of limited keywords you are allowed to add. You only get a limited number of keywords to add which is 6 for printed books and 8 for eBooks. Your best bet is to Google the key words you pick and find out which of those words are viewed the most. The keywords need to be something that are viewed a lot, simply because those are the words that a person would normally put in the search box to find your topic or genre. It is more complicated than that, and I recommend you research getting the best keywords for your book/title and genre. As the example above, the keywords for the title about cabins: home renovation, wooden houses, contractors, how to, building, DYI could be used. Two words put together as one thought count as one keyword. If you are unsure of whether it is one or two, the best thing you can do is speak to a real person in the publishing company or Amazon if you are publishing with Createspace or KDP, and they will tell you if you have the right amount or too many keywords. Keep in mind that the summary/description should have all of these keywords, because when the search engine does its work, it will match the keyword with your summary and the chances of your book coming up are higher the more overlap there is of the keywords. Remember, you are competing with other books on the same or similar topic so the more hits you get for one keyword helps in your book being displayed on the first few pages of a search engine. On Amazon, the review rating also affects how your book will display, which is another thing to consider when you are new and want to get 4 to 5 star reviews from people not related to by last name. You will have to address this after the book is posted online in circulation and you are trying to keep it in the queue of the search results.

Fifth: The last thing is to make any corrections once you get a printed proof and resubmit the manuscript or cover, whichever needs correction. Make sure you read and look at every page for printing errors, like extra gaps in spacing, missing information, etc. Get another proof, or if you don't need to, finalize the process and the company will continue with the final publishing process and put your book in the distributor channels online. For print on demand books, this means that a bookstore has your book in their online system and someone can order the book at a store. In other words, your book will not be put on a bookshelf unless you have an agent and contract, the book hits the bestseller, or you personally buy books and have a book signing event out of your pocket. On the other side, your book will be displayed online and people will see it on Amazon and other distributing channels for a time period of about a month or more depending on the number of reviews from readers. In other words, the review ratings will dictate how long the book will be up on the long list of books with the similar genre. Newly published books are automatically left on the first few pages of a site for about a month if not less. After that period, the book's review rating will either keep it posted on the top listed or be pushed down the queue, and unless someone searches specifically for your title and/or name, your book will display on page 10-100 of a search results, and chances are your book will not be seen and not sell. I am telling you this here in this section, so you will understand how important it is to have good keywords. Important to have an attack plan on how to get your review ratings high, and how you should not be down trodden if your book doesn't become a success; meaning you sell less and not make up for your cost in making the book. If sales is your only goal, then you need to have an attack plan for marketing, a stellar book cover that catches the eye from a viewing of a thumbnail and continue to speak to people and get them to write reviews for you.

Sixth: If you find a problem with your book afterward, you can fix it, but it will cost you time to go through the process again, and in the meantime, the book you did publish will be available for a time as you republish. This might not be a big deal, but you might end up with an unwanted delay and any erroneous information on the summary or bio might linger online, until you fix it.

Seventh: Kindle Direct, Createspace, and Lulu accounts allow you to monitor your sales, and also give you tax information when needed. All other companies do the same and if you get a company that does not track your book's financial information, I would stay away from them.

Attention to detail is important and reading your online information is never a waste of time. Your marketing strategy is also as important. The best method without an agent, is to get people to rate your book (give you a review) on Amazon or wherever you publish. You can ask people you don't know like in websites that exchange reviews, or people you do know. The thing is you need to make sure the reviewer gives you a good review in what is said, not just the number of stars that are given. It is recommended you give a premade review (made by you) to your friends or associates that know you and just have them post it in their name. Of course don't give all your friends the same review. You need to make each review unique and address the strengths of the book to mirror the book description if possible. A 4 or 5 star, here and there, Having all 5 stars is possible, but not normal for new books. In time your new readers will give you their reviews which hopefully will keep your book in the top 20 listing on Amazon. The longer the listing, the more chance of readers seeing your book and getting it. If you don't get reviews, your book will be dropped off the top viewed and be lost in a long list of books. When someone types in one of your keywords, they will see someone else's book because they have more good reviews than you do or their book just listed. Usually your new listing of a book will be on there from two to seven days, maybe longer if you pay for a marketing package. Otherwise the reader will have to surf the list of books for more than 8 web pages which most readers never do; or they have to type in your name in order to see your book(s). This is where an author website helps which can help direct exposure to Amazon specific pages of your book(s).

Having said that, there are online courses that help you learn how to market, publish, and create your book. Fostering Success is one website company where you can pay from $60 to $300 and they give you courses on how to market your book on social media, and much more. Of course you have to pay, which might be worth it depending on how much help you need or if your strength is not in promoting your book. It could be because you don't have time to market your book, so going with online resources like this might or might not be for you.

eBooks: are different from printed books, because they have a different formatting system and are easier to market. The publishing company will instruct you how it should be formatted. KDP has a good video on how to do this, by using the paragraph styles in Microsoft Word; using Normal, Heading 1, Heading 2, and Heading 3. You also have to get rid of the page numbers and table of content if you have one. The Heading styles will create your chapters. Basically the body of the text needs to be in normal style. The Title page Heading 1, and chapters are in heading 2 and 3 respectfully. I already talked about the typeface which should be one that is compatible with the publisher. Other than that, the advantage of publishing an eBook is that your proof is instant, and you can read your final proof as a download. It will at the most cost $1 if not free for the proof. Your eBooks also usually have a 90-100% royalty, so if your eBook costs $3.95, you will get that amount per sale if not close to all. It might not sound like a lot, but it is if you sell 1,000 or more in a month. In addition, you don't really have to have an ISBN for an eBook. The publisher will assign a number to it when you pay for the publishing which is around $90 with KDP (Kindle Direct Publishing). To be on the safe side to make sure my books could be sent to all distributors and other companies, I bought my own ISBNs for my eBooks. It's up to you on the extra cost, but if you don't have an ISBN or plan on only writing one or two books and have a tight budget, then going with the publishing company's ISBN might be better for you since it will be cheaper for one or a few eBooks.

Chapter 5

❊ --- ❊

Traditional Publishing

On a practical note; your writing has to be very good to get a traditional publisher to pick up your book, OR you will happen to know someone who knows someone. There are books out there that are in circulation, and you wonder how the heck did this person get this book in the store? Book agents are people whose work is to get a publishing company to take on a book for sales. Sales of the book and to some degree the author is what makes it known or not known. Famous people are examples of this business. Anyone who makes headline news with controversy is up for a signing, and the traditional publishing company will probably try to get a piece of the action. Most people who, like OJ Simpson, didn't grow up thinking I want to become a famous author or bestseller. An agent approached OJ with an offer from a company to publish a book for him, willingly taking on the task of formatting, editing, and printing the book. The only thing the author had to do was tell the story and give the company permission to print it as it was written in the final form. Chances are that you are not famous at present, so getting a traditional publisher to take on your book will be by showing them your writing is exceptionally brilliant, or an agent pushes your work in the hopes that it will be big.

Knowing people helps in this effort, so socializing with other authors, writers, and readers on social or writing based websites might give you an opening to show off your work. The other way of getting an agent to read your work is to actively search for agents in your genre. Authorconnect.com is one website where you can find agents and send them an email to include a sample of your first one to three chapters. The agent will tell you if they are interested or tell you why they are not interested. Usually, it will be because the first 10 pages of the book didn't catch their eye or interest. Like I said, the book has to be brilliantly written, and if it doesn't have that hook, then they would rather wait for someone that does which will have a higher chance of getting picked up by a traditional publisher.

An agent gets you inside the publishing company. Or at least is actively trying to get your book published through the company. So why is this important? Royalties are different in self-published and traditional publishing. There is normally more exposure of your book through a traditional publishing company, because the company is actively promoting your book at their expense so the more successful you become, the more money they make. In self publishing, there is no high investment on the self-publishing company's part to actively promote your book which may or may not be of good quality. The royalty percentage might be higher on average in self-publishing, but the chance of many sales is dependent on your book and marketing system which is not being advertised by the publishing company as strong as a traditional company. In addition, the focus is on quantity of sales for all books, not just yours. So the more books the self-publishing companies produce, the more of a chance that one book will explode and make them money. So you are subject to the system, and this is where you have to decide how to tackle the problem of how you go about writing and publishing your book. Don't get me wrong. It is not all about money. Publishing companies do want you to be successful for more than just money. The book industry in the past used to be an arena where paper piles of written works were overwhelming and good writers were not recognized because of the limitations by the companies and industry. Self-publishing has opened up many people to write and the industry to explode like never before.

With online publishing and eBooks, there is a higher chance that your book exploding on the internet is higher than trying to get an agent to sell your first book to a large conglomerate publishing machine. However, there is always the chance that an agent will take up your cause. So I would recommend you go with self-publishing, after you attempted at least once to get feedback from one or two agents. Also, just because you publish an ebook, doesn't mean that you can't hold off from constantly communicating or trying to correspond with an agent, and if your ebook does great, you can try again to get an agent for a printed book version. This time you will hopefully have many good reviews from New York Times type of critics, and chances are that you will get an agent and move into the traditional arena. In the end, you will have hopefully been exposed to what you like about self-publishing and stay there or move into traditional and find it better or worse than what you thought. Moving back to self-publishing will not lessen your success, but might enhance it if you are well known.

Chapter 6

❋ --- ❋

Process Approach to Writing

I f you are under the age of twenty, you are probably familiar with what is called the process approach to writing. This teaching method is recently and widely used in middle and high school curriculums for learning how to write. The process approach to writing is broken down into three steps: pre-writing, focusing ideas, and evaluating, structuring and editing. Your English teacher might not have told you what they were doing when trying to get you to write an essay or story, but the concept is sound and relates to writing a book. I didn't say that you should use this method to write a book or long story. The reason is that this method might help you write a book, but if you analyze the process sort of speaking, it teaches you how to write better not how to write a book. People will tell you to relax, write, and put thoughts on paper, then after the thoughts are on paper, change it to make it coherent, and lastly edit the work so it is mechanically free of errors.

The process to writing is similar in that it tells you to come up with ideas for your story, this is the pre-writing step. Brainstorm the ideas, to include names for characters, personalities, sub plots, conflict, settings, and how the conflict is resolved or not. All of this can be in your head or on paper, or both. The second step is to put things together and arrange on paper what happens first, second, third, and so on. In a classroom setting, you have input from other students and the teacher. In your home environment, you have other writers and friends who can help you question and improve on your characters, plots, and so on. The third step is to actually put the story on paper by writing it. Not worrying about proper grammar, spelling, or punctuation. It is your first rough draft.

The idea is if you write enough stories this process will become easier and when you write your rough draft, there are less errors and the ideas are put together better. SO when it is time to edit your work, your story flows smoothly, your friends give you feedback, or just people online or in person can help you improve your writing style and fix any errors in the story. An exaggerated example is if John's leg is broken in a fall, then a week later John should not be sprinting down the street in a race later in the story, unless he has some super regenerating power or reason to be fully healthy in a week. Names might be mislabeled with dialogue, and all the errors to include mechanics (grammar, spelling, punctuation, tenses) need to be addressed in this last step. In the end you end up with a final story.

I say story, because unfortunately, the process that you probably went through in school taught you how to write a semi-story; more likely how to write an essay or paper that is focused on a second person present tense instructional or controversial topic. What you are not taught is how to tell a story, but fear not. The concept like I said is sound, and as long as you modify the process, you can make it work.

The pre-writing step should be focused on what you want your book to say. The main idea first; then figure out what the sub plots are. If you want to write about a girl who finds out she is a werewolf and is coming to an age where she needs to decide to follow her estranged family or fight against the family who stole her at birth, then you have a starting point for your book. If you want to write about how to make ceramic and glass figurines out of your garage, you just need to come up with the main figurine(s) to show case as your teaching point, and probably some main tools and equipment used for the construction of a possibly lucrative business or hobby.

Step two is putting the ideas together into an outline. Many authors use outlines to help them stay focused on the story and timeline. Some authors don't do this. I for one have the basic outline in my head for the superhero series and just know that one event needs to happen before another does as I write. I do use an outline for the other books I have written. Whichever way you do it, the intent is to not go down rabbit holes like some authors do and go off into tangents in the middle of a conflict and the reader is thrown around left and right before returning to the main story. If you have read Stephen King books, you know what I am talking about. It is not common, but it happens, and it is usually because the author is not following an outline on paper, or has a mental storyline which he or she changes as inspiration hits or misses. I have been told that I have gone off in tangents in my superhero books with subplots. They fail to understand is that the subplots intertwine with the other books in the series, so what a critic might say is bad about book two, is not when the reader sees the plot unfold in book three or four. This is not the best method in writing a book, but in a series of books, it does work well as long as the subplots are not way out there. An example of not connecting the dots in subplots would be to write about a murder, and out of nowhere a subplot comes up about an artist who wins the lotto; and because of that he moves outs of state and isn't killed next. But you never read or hear about the artist who you spent one or two chapters on and in the current or future books.

This does not mean that everything you write has to be important enough to be in your book. As for the writing style, you should refrain from repeating yourself. You can get rid of repetition, like saying "I hate that", John hatefully (or angrily) said. This type of writing is wasted words and you should focus on the story as a whole and use lines in dialogue to complement John, like John sat pouting at the floor. In addition, if you write about a colorful character and your audience loves that character so much, that on the second to last chapter, the character is killed off, then why did you make that character? Well, it is your story and I try to avoid killing off characters, but it happens as in real life, but the point is to make an impression of how a society is, how characters interact with their surroundings, and most importantly how descriptive you can be on everything you write. Because the story is not about if you said only the essentials, it is about bringing in the reader into the world you created and make them a part of that world.

Step three should be where you focus on the mechanics and getting as much feedback as you have been getting through the construction of your story. Your Stylewriter type software, and eye-ball editors (to include you) should be hitting this story hard. Once you have a good feeling that it is the final manuscript, you are that much closer to publishing.

The next part is to finalize the cover art, book description, and publishing details on who you are using like Createspace or Lulu, and technical requirements (ISBNS, formats, etc). Getting feedback from your friends and online assistance is important through all the steps, even after your book is being distributed online and in stores.

You are never done if you want to promote your book. If you don't care about promoting your book, then just sit back and do nothing. Chances are that you do something and not sit around, and I recommend you talk to people; spread the word online and in person about your book(s). Use any and all marketing tools you can get a hold of, free or expensive ones if you have the money. If you get average 3 star reviews or 1 star reviews, look at them and move on. Improve your writing because you want to, not because a person didn't like that you can't write like Shakespeare, Token, or Hallmark. You will know if your writing is good enough to leave a good impression. This is normally when other writers tell you so, but more importantly, when the majority of readers tell you they like your writing. There are bestseller authors that have hundreds of 1 star reviews and several hundreds of 4 and 5 star reviews on a book. What does that mean? The author has enough followers that it is probably not one of the books that made bestseller, but at one point the author wrote something right, and is still selling books with 1-5 star reviews. So keep writing and don't stop at one book. Write a short book of 50 pages, or a 1,000 page novel, but keep writing. You will see that your writing will improve and be easier to do the more you write. In like fashion you will be a success, just keep at it.

Author Notes

❈ --- ❈

I covered many topics and details, but there are a few things I didn't mention about eBook publishing. The normal formatting typefaces you put into a word document are not compatible with an epub format. Epub format is the final format an eBook goes through to be an eBook. The styles of normal, heading 1, heading 2, and heading 3 is a simple concept to learn. However, the hanging letter in your word document will not transfer. So if you are expecting to have a bolded large letter, cap drop, to introduce a chapter, that will not happen unless you make the first letter, in this case for this chapter the letter I needs to be a larger font and within the paragraph. So you would write it by deleting the hanging letters and replacing them with a larger font of that letter in the paragraph - an example below:

I covered many topics and details, but…

If you don't bold or make the font larger, it's okay. Your chapter will start with regular text, like the rest of the body. I made it a point to bold it, enlarge it, and not indent to give the reader a strong starting point of a chapter. If you don't like the look, play with it. You can view your eBook proof when KDP or whoever is publishing your book allows you. Make the changes to fonts and see what you like, this includes line spacing. If all fails and you don't like the look, you can pay the company to format it for you which will probably cost between \$30-\$100. It all depends on the publishing company. This includes the bookmarks which is your chapters or navigation. Note: chapters or breaks are automatically populated when you create the correct style types in the document.

Kindle Direct Publishing has an extensive list of resources to create your cover and specific books which include children books and textbooks. If you have the illustrations, you just need to make sure they are within the required specifications and of course make sure you are not violating any copyright laws by using someone else's illustrations. If you don't go with KDP, just make sure you follow the directions of the publishing process. I focus on KDP because it is by far the easiest, quickest, and best resource to self-publish an eBook. In addition, it is easy to track your marketing and success of you eBook on a regular basis.

Lastly, selling your eBook for less than \$2 might work short-term, but if you know that your book will sell because it is that good, go for a higher price. Normally, you will know on your third or more published book. How will you know? If you have established followers, then go a little higher in price, but not too much. The intent is not to squeeze money out of people. The intent is to get paid for a book that is worth the money because you spent the time and work into making a very good book. Normally, unknown authors tend to sell books very cheap as low as free to \$0.99 so they can be known and get their expertise out to the world. In time, the hope is to get a following and expand your writing and enjoyment for yourself and others. In addition, the price you choose will be reduced in time, which is normal for books that are in the market for a certain amount of time, and are sold used or with a reduced price by the middlemen of the market.

I appreciate your interest and hope this book has helped you in writing, planning, and launching your dreams into reality.

Published books:

Jesus and the Paint on the Wall (2012)

Doomsday Prepping and Survival, From Civil Disturbances
to Biblical Proportions (2014)

A Superhero Epic Series

Creator (2004, 2014)

He Is Known as Ego (2006, 2014)

Guild Without a Name (2014)

The Galaxy Is Ours (2014)

Masterminds (2014)

Superhumans From the Past (2016)

Ultimate Assassins (2016)